21st Century
Basic Skills
Library

THE WORLD AROUND US
LAKES

by Cecilia Minden, PhD

Cherry Lake Publishing • Ann Arbor, Michigan

2

Published in the United States of America
by Cherry Lake Publishing
Ann Arbor, Michigan
www.cherrylakepublishing.com

Photo Credits: Cover and page 1, ©iStockphoto.com/thanialex;
page 4, ©Kevin Eaves/Shutterstock, Inc.; page 6, ©Ronald Summers/
Shutterstock, Inc.; page 8, ©Daniel Petrescu/Shutterstock, Inc.; page 10,
©Mogens Trolle/Shutterstock, Inc.; page 12, ©Vilmos Varga/Shutterstock,
Inc.; page 14, ©Yanik Chauvin; page 16, ©Noonie/Dreamstime.com;
page 18, ©Sebastien Burel/Shutterstock, Inc.; page 20, ©iStockphoto.
com/Sportstock

Library of Congress Cataloging-in-Publication Data
Minden, Cecilia.
  The world around us: lakes/by Cecilia Minden.
     p. cm.—(21st century basic skills library level 2)
  Includes bibliographical references and index.
  ISBN-13: 978-1-60279-859-5 (lib. bdg.)
  ISBN-10: 1-60279-859-1 (lib. bdg.)
  1. Lakes—Juvenile literature. I. Title. II. Series.
  GB1603.8.M56 2010
  551.48'2—dc22   2009048585

Cherry Lake Publishing would like to acknowledge
the work of The Partnership for 21st Century Skills.
Please visit www.21stcenturyskills.org for more information.

Printed in the United States of America
Corporate Graphics Inc.
July 2010
CLFA07

TABLE OF CONTENTS

What Do We Know About Lakes?

A **lake** is a big **body of water**.

There is land all around it.

Some lakes have been here for a long time.

Other lakes are **man-made**.

People may put a **dam** across a river.

This makes a big lake.

Most lakes are filled with **freshwater**.

Rain and snow keep lakes full of water. If there is no rain or snow, lakes can dry up.

Who Lives in Lakes?

Animals use lakes for food and water.

Water feels good on a hot day.

Lakes have many kinds of fish.

Big lakes have the biggest fish!

What Can You Do at a Lake?

Lakes are good places to have fun.

Many people like water sports.

You can sail in a boat.

You can **water-ski** behind a fast boat!

Other people like to camp or hike.

There is always something fun to do at the lake.

What will you do at the lake?

Find Out More

BOOK

Bekkering, Annalise. *The Great Lakes*. New York: Weigl
    Publishers, 2008.

WEB SITE

Lake Habitat
www.hamiltonnature.org/habitats/lake/lake.htm
Learn more about lakes and the animals and plants that live
in and near them.

Glossary

body of water (BOD-ee UHV WAW-tur) a large amount of water such as a lake, river, or ocean

dam (DAM) a wall built across a river to hold back water

freshwater (FRESH-waw-tur) water in a lake or river that is not salty

lake (LAYK) a large body of water surrounded by land

man-made (MAN-MAYD) something created by people

water-ski (WAW-tur-SKEE) to travel over water on two long boards called skis

Home and School Connection

Use this list of words from the book to help your child become a better reader. Word games and writing activities can help beginning readers reinforce literacy skills.

a	dry	know	river
about	fast	lake	sail
across	feels	lakes	snow
all	filled	land	some
always	fish	like	something
and	food	lives	sports
animals	for	long	the
are	freshwater	makes	there
around	full	man-made	this
at	fun	many	time
been	good	may	to
behind	have	most	up
big	here	no	use
biggest	hike	of	water
boat	hot	on	water-ski
body	if	or	we
camp	in	other	what
can	is	people	who
dam	it	places	will
day	keep	put	with
do	kinds	rain	you

Index

About the Author

Cecilia Minden is the former Director of the Language and Literacy Program at the Harvard Graduate School of Education. She currently works as a literacy consultant for school and library publishers and is the author of more than 100 books for children.